Special f...

Detailed pictures for added interest and discussion

Wider vocabulary, reinforced through repetition

What do chefs do?
Chefs work in kitchens. They prepare and cook food.

little kitchen

I work in a little kitchen.

8

big kitchen

prepared food

I work in a big kitchen.

cooked food

Fresh food
Some chefs grow food to cook.

I grow fruit and vegetables.

vegetables

fruit

32

Chefs get fresh fruit, vegetables, meat and fish at food markets, too.

meat

fish

food market

33

Longer sentences

Captions and labels clarify information

Educational Consultant: Geraldine Taylor
Book Banding Consultant: Kate Ruttle
Subject Consultant: Tom Cenci

LADYBIRD BOOKS

UK | USA | Canada | Ireland | Australia
India | New Zealand | South Africa

Ladybird Books is part of the Penguin Random House group of companies
whose addresses can be found at global.penguinrandomhouse.com.

www.penguin.co.uk www.puffin.co.uk www.ladybird.co.uk

First published 2019
001

Copyright © Ladybird Books Ltd, 2019

Printed in China

A CIP catalogue record for this book is available from the British Library

ISBN: 978-0-241-36111-5

All correspondence to
Ladybird Books
Penguin Random House Children's Books
80 Strand, London WC2R 0RL

I am a Chef

Written by Zoë Clarke
Illustrated by Nina de Polonia-Nill

Contents

What do chefs do?   8

Chefs' hats   10

Training to be a chef   12

Kitchen equipment   14

Slips and trips   16

Junior chef   18

Station chef   20

So many chefs!   22

Pastry chef   24

Sous chef   26

Head chef   28

Menu plan   30

Fresh food   32

Big parties   34

School cook   36

Hospital chef   38

Ship's cook   40

You can be a chef!   42

Picture glossary   44

Index   46

I am a Chef quiz   47

What do chefs do?

Chefs work in kitchens. They prepare and cook food.

little kitchen

I work in a little kitchen.

Chefs' hats

Chefs have a hat, a jacket, safe shoes and an apron.

hat

jacket

The chef in the big hat is in charge.

I am the head chef.
I am in charge!

big hat

apron

safe shoes

Training to be a chef
Some people go to chef school.

We are training at chef school.

12

Chefs train so they can prepare and cook good food.

We will be good chefs!

Kitchen equipment

Chefs train to be safe with kitchen equipment, too.

sharp knife

Sharp knives are put away safely.

Ovens are hot! Chefs have oven cloths.

hot oven

oven
cloth

Slips and trips
Chefs clean up, so no one slips.

16

The kitchen must be tidy, so no one trips.

I will tidy the kitchen.

Junior chef

If you want to be a chef, you must train as a junior chef.

chopped
vegetables

Junior chefs chop and prepare the food for cooking!

They help to prepare sauces
for the station chefs.

station chef

sauces

Station chef

Station chefs prepare one food all the time. They can cook meat, fish, vegetables and sauces.

meat

I prepare all the meat!

fish

So many chefs!

In a big kitchen, there are many station chefs.

I cook fried food.

fried food

23

Pastry chef

Pastry chefs are in charge
of baking.

bread oven

They prepare and bake the bread.

24

Then, they bake the cakes and pastries.

cakes

pastries

Sous chef

The sous chef is in charge of the kitchen. They look at the station chefs' work.

Sous chefs will help out if there is a lot of work.

I will help out!

27

Head chef

Head chefs tell the station chefs what to cook.

They get food for the chefs
to cook in the kitchen.

The chefs will cook all
this fresh food.

Menu plan

The head chef plans menus
with the sous chef.

People look at the menus and
see what food they would like.

What would you
like to have?

I would like the fried
fish with vegetables.

Chefs get fresh fruit, vegetables, meat and fish at food markets, too.

meat

fish

food market

Big parties
Some chefs cook food for big parties.

I have chopped all these vegetables.

I have cooked a big fish.

I have made a big cake.

I have made pastries.

35

School cook

A chef in a school is called a cook.

School cooks prepare vegetables, fish, meat, salads and fresh fruit.

I cook food for many people.

Hospital chef

There are many people to cook for in a hospital, too.

I cook food for the people in this hospital.

Hospital chefs prepare and cook food to help people get well.

Ship's cook

The chef on a ship is called the ship's cook.

I make food for all the people on this ship!

The cook can get fresh food
from the market.

fresh food

market

You can be a chef!

You can . . .

. . . grow
fruit and
vegetables.

. . . plan
a menu.

. . . help
prepare
the food.

I am
a chef!

. . . help cook
the food.

. . . have a
big party.

43

Picture glossary

 bake

 chef

 cook

 equipment

 fish

 fruit

 kitchen

 knives

 market

 meat

 oven

 vegetables

Index

bake   24, 25
chef school   12
cook   8, 13, 20, 22, 23, 28, 29,
                    32, 34, 36, 37, 38, 39, 43
equipment   14
fish   20, 21, 31, 33, 34
fruit   32, 33, 37, 42
head chef   11, 28, 30
hospital chef   38, 39
junior chef   18,
kitchen   8, 9, 14, 17, 22, 26, 29
market   33, 41
meat   20, 33, 37
menu   30, 31, 42
party   34, 43
pastry chef   24
school cook   36, 37
ship's cook   40
station chef   19, 20, 22, 26, 28
sous chef   26, 27, 30
vegetables   18, 20, 31, 32, 33, 34,
                    37, 42